Dedication

Your life, love and legacy lives on forever in
the hearts of those who love you.
I will always do my best to make you proud.
Keep resting in sweet peace *Queen Mother*.

Mrs. Carolyn B. Worthy
1947 – 2006

***You fought a good fight, you finished your course
and you kept the faith.***
(II Timothy 4:7)

Dedication

This book is dedicated as well to these strong individuals whom I am blessed to know and love. They have kept the faith and the wherewithal after being diagnosed with the big "C" word. They continue to hold their heads high and they are always showing appreciation and love to others.

I love you dearly ***Angela D. Tooley King, Valerie Hunter-Moye and Charles Kollock.*** I speak your names in love and respect. Giving you flowers while you can see, read and appreciate them. Please hang in there because He was wounded for our transgressions, He was bruised for our iniquities: the chastisement of our peace was upon Him; and with His stripes you are healed. *(Isaiah 53:5)*

Angela Tooley King (Left) Valerie Hunter-Moye (Middle) Charles Kollock (Right)

Table of Contents

Don't Ignore The Signs
(Your Life is Speaking)

Don't Ignore The Signs

(Your Life is Speaking)

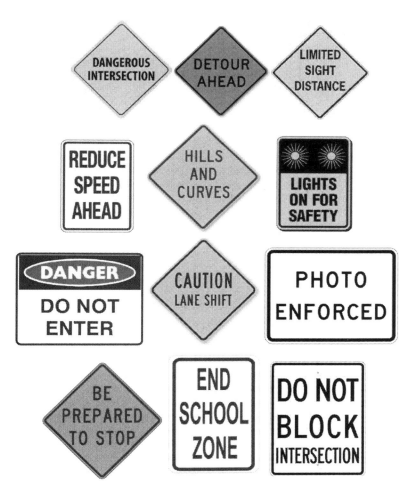

Introduction

Signs are everywhere. All around us, we have the necessary information to make proper decisions and act in the most effective and efficient ways possible. We must make a conscious effort to slow down and read the signs. When we take the time to observe our surroundings and take heed of the warnings, we allow ourselves access to the wisdom that is around us.

The rules of the road are regularly posted everywhere for all to see. If we obey the guidelines laid out by the collection of road signs, the roads are a safer place for all who share the roads together. Life is no different in this regard and oftentimes our lives are impacted significantly when we do not heed the warnings attached to the signs we encounter in our lives.

In *Don't Ignore the Signs*, author Shunda Brown encourages readers to tune in and take notice of the signs in their own lives. The signs on the road mimic the signs of life, as signage is strategically recycled from one medium to the next. If you miss the signs or ignore them, you could miss the directions, suggestions, and advice, which directly or indirectly affects your life. Look out, look in, look up, and look down. A lot can be learned from a simple look around. Keep your eye out for the signals of life and choose wisely after you have taken stock of your surroundings.

Inside *Don't Ignore the Signs*, the author takes a twenty-first century glimpse into some of the daily "life" signs that we see. Such as, No U-Turn, Stop, Expect Delays, Merge, Do Not Enter, Slow, One-Way, Wrong Way, Road Closed Ahead, Stay in Lane, and Dangerous Curve Head, to name a few.

Sit down, buckle up, and settle in for the ride. The signs will guide you the rest of the way from here, all the way to your final destination of truth and wisdom.

Chapter 1
No U Turn

Sometimes as we are traveling on life's highways, we realize that we need to go in the opposite direction. Perhaps you have missed a street that you meant to turn on or maybe your vehicle's GPS malfunctioned and you suddenly realize you are driving in the wrong direction. Whenever you need to change the direction you are driving, a U-turn might be necessary. Word to the wise, watch for signage that will inform you if it is legal or not to make a U-turn.

If there is a NO U-TURN sign posted, you must use wisdom and practice patience to get to your destination. Some U-turns can cause traffic problems and accidents. Be mindful of this when it comes to your own life. You can change your mind, you can decide not to attend an event, you can change careers, you have every right to change direction, however, paying attention to the signs in your life will save you time from going in the wrong direction to avoid having to make a U-turn. Pay attention to what your life is saying to you.

If something does not feel quite right, that is usually your gut feeling giving you a warning sign that danger could be close.

A U-turn on a crowded highway or street can cause a major traffic accident. Think about it, have you ever noticed that when there is a NO U-turn sign posted, usually not far from this sign is clearance for the U-turn you need to make. Patience is required on life's journey as well as common sense.

When you are not attentive to what your life is saying to you, you will more than likely waste time, energy and money, all because you failed to see the No U-turn sign glaring you in the face. Stay focused when you are in the driver's seat of your destiny and remember that sometimes life does offer chances for do-overs and sometimes it does not.

No U Turn
Write to the Point: Journal Space
(Please use this page to jot down your thoughts after reading this chapter)

Chapter 2
STOP

If we are completely honest with ourselves, we can admit that there have been times and instances where we thought, "I need to stop". The first thought that comes to mind is the wasted time and energy on things, situations and people that could have been prevented had we paid closer attention to the signs that were exhibited. Sometimes we turn a blind eye for peace sake. Sometimes we simply ignore all of the warning signs as it relates to life's truth markers. These are those signs that let us know when something is just not right.

In this chapter, I wanted to share reminders of things that we need to take inventory of in our lives and if it applies **STOP**! Take inventory of what is going on in your life. Pay attention to what you felt was just fleeting thoughts. Stop. Pray. Listen. Think. Write it down. Journal. Get positive counsel and make the necessary changes you need to enjoy the life you are blessed with. This certainly does not mean that things will be perfect (they will not be) but making changes in your life will certainly make things easier for you to handle.

On the following list, you will find the most common things that need to be STOPPED right away:

Some may apply to you or someone you know for sure.

- ✓ Stop waiting for your ship to come in, learn how to swim
- ✓ Stop speaking negativity over your life
- ✓ Stop pretending to like people when you really don't
- ✓ Stop settling for less when you know you deserve better
- ✓ Stop pretending to be happy
- ✓ Stop trying to please people
- ✓ Stop expecting from others what you are not willing to give
- ✓ Stop whining and complaining
- ✓ Stop playing games with people's lives and emotions
- ✓ Stop hanging around people who bring out the worst in you
- ✓ Stop singing the blues
- ✓ Stop putting up with people's mistreatment of you
- ✓ Stop making excuses for people's bad behavior
- ✓ Stop working and not taking vacations
- ✓ Stop living in the past
- ✓ Stop being petty and messy
- ✓ Stop being selfish
- ✓ Stop being lazy
- ✓ Stop being stingy
- ✓ Stop and smell the roses
- ✓ Stop in the name of love
- ✓ Stop allowing people to use you
- ✓ Stop working just for a paycheck
- ✓ Stop playing the victim to situations you created

✓ Stop blaming others for your mistakes

✓ Stop trying to fit in where you don't belong

✓ Stop doing things you know are not good for your health

✓ Stop lying to yourself and others

✓ Stop trying to impress people you don't like

✓ Stop hanging around people who have no goals or dreams

✓ Stop eating unhealthy

✓ Stop allowing people to drain you of your good energy

✓ Stop procrastinating your life away

✓ Stop robbing Peter to pay Paul (they are bankrupt!)

✓ Stop allowing people to hold you hostage to past mistakes

This is a starter list of things that need you or someone you know may need to put a STOP to! *Don't Ignore the Signs!* You know when it is time to move on. Listen to your heart, read the sign twice if need be and keep it moving. Your destiny awaits you and your best days are on the horizon. Listen to what the signs are saying to you.

STOP
Write to the Point: Journal Space
(Please use this page to jot down your thoughts after reading this chapter)

_____

_____

_____

_____

_____

_____

_____

_____

_____

_____

_____

_____

_____

_____

_____

Chapter 3
DO NOT ENTER

When a DO NOT ENTER sign is posted, it is usually to warn drivers that they should not travel in that direction. Either on side streets or major highways, this sign is a popular warning sign that screams "Don't Go that Way!" yet in life, when some people see this sign, they tend to ignore it and end up in a world of trouble that could have been avoided.

Going in the wrong area or direction can cause you to crash into oncoming traffic. It could be that this sign is there to prevent you from harming yourself or someone else. This sign could be warning you that certain people are not good for you. It could also be a reminder that you need to take your time and really get to know the people you have chosen to sit on the front row of your life. ***Do Not Enter*** almost sounds like a command. Don't spend your wheels having to re-route your entire life because you failed to take heed to the warning signs along the way. Stay away from the things that you know will not add value to your life. If people cannot compliment your life, please do not allow them to complicate it.

DO NOT ENTER
Write to the Point: Journal Space
(Please use this page to jot down your thoughts after reading this chapter)

Chapter 4
SLOW

Another road sign that gives warning for drivers to pay more attention is the SLOW one. Slow means just that, time to hit the brakes and reduce your speed. Enjoy the ride while taking time to live in the moments you are blessed with. Put your cell phones down, get off social media and take time to acknowledge how truly blessed you are.

You cannot learn valuable life lessons if you are always rushing or always in a hurry. Slow down and take time to let others know you appreciate them. Do nice things (flowers, dinner, cards in the mail, surprise telephone call) to show them that you really care. Observe your surroundings. Take it all in and be grateful for the life you are blessed with. Don't take living well for granted. Things could always be worse. Slow down, look around and take note of every sign that your life is showing you. Some things just cannot be rushed or microwaved.

SLOW
Write to the Point: Journal Space
(Please use this page to jot down your thoughts after reading this chapter)

Chapter 5

WRONG WAY

Have you ever wasted time, energy and money on things because you were not paying attention? Have you ever bought something but in your haste, you find when you get it home, it is not what you expected? Have you ever ended up in a place or situation and wondered to yourself, "how in the world did I get here?" Have you ever regretted meeting certain people?

Have you ever felt bad after having said "yes" when you know you should have said "no"? If you answered yes to either of these questions, it is probably because you did not pay closer attention to the sign that said WRONG WAY. Had you noticed the sign and obeyed it, you would have gotten to your destination on time, less frustrated and ready to enjoy yourself.

Wrong way travelers can find themselves in places they were not supposed to be in simply because they were distracted while driving and not paying attention to the signs that forewarned you to avoid traveling in a certain direction. Life is precious and should be lived well every single day.

Stop ignoring the warning signs in your life and stop driving in the wrong direction. Pray for direction and guidance so that you do not end up lost and frustrated. The signs in your life are talking, don't you hear them? Don't be persuaded by naysayers and energy vampires to participate in things that are not on your agenda. Don't let them beat you being GREAT! Stop listening to back seat drivers and pay closer attention to your life's signs. Wrong way driving can cost you years of your life and you do not have time to start over when you could have gotten it right the first time around.

WRONG WAY
Write to the Point: Journal Space
(Please use this page to jot down your thoughts after reading this chapter)

_____

_____

_____

_____

_____

_____

_____

_____

_____

_____

_____

_____

_____

_____

Chapter 6
STAY IN LANE

Recently, the state of Georgia passed a "hands free" law which states that all drivers operating a motor vehicle on any highway of this state are prohibited from holding or supporting, a wireless telecommunications device or stand-alone electronic device.

The law also states that also prohibited is writing, sending or reading any text-based communication, including a text message, instant message, e-mail or internet data and watching, recording, or broadcasting a video or movie. Prior to this law being passed, distracted drivers were easily identifiable by how reckless they were driving.

When drivers get out of their lanes, it causes accidents. The sign posted reads STAY IN LANE, which is a clear indication and warning that we must pay attention and focus on the roads we are traveling on. Stay in lane also could mean to do what you have been gifted and called by God to do. Stop allowing others to cause you to crash because you are doing things that you do not feel comfortable or qualified to do. For example, if you are a good public speaker, you should busy yourselves with that type career.

Do not let folks trick you into getting out of your lane and embarrassing yourself. Stay in lane could also be defined as being respectful of people's privacy. I would add that some people just need to "mind their business". Take time to attend to your affairs and less time trying to figure out what is going on with others. There is already enough on your plate to handle. Stay in your own lane!

STAY IN LANE
Write to the Point: Journal Space
(Please use this page to jot down your thoughts after reading this chapter)

_____

_____

_____

_____

_____

_____

_____

_____

_____

_____

_____

_____

_____

_____

Chapter 7
PROCEED WITH CAUTION

This sign reminds drivers to slow down and stay alert wile proceeding with caution. It also warns drivers of impending danger ahead. As the driver of your destiny, be sure to buckle up and prepare yourself for the day that lies ahead. Start each day with an attitude of gratitude. Jot things down that you want to accomplish that day. Set aside time to meditate, pray and remind yourself that you are going to have a great day. Do this and be intentional and firm when speaking positivity into your morning.

Proceed with caution also could mean to take heed and to watch out for dangerous situations. This warning is not intended to make drivers nervous or fearful but to remind them to take your time and travel safely. Take the necessary time and steps to get to know what you are embarking upon before you jump in headfirst. Take time to get to know people. Take time to do the research if you are interested in changing careers. Do your homework. Don't be in a rush to get projects completed and later discover that you missed an important step because you were in a hurry. Proceed with caution and pray about it all.

PROCEED WITH CAUTION
Write to the Point: Journal Space
(Please use this page to jot down your thoughts after reading this chapter)

_____

_____

_____

_____

_____

_____

_____

_____

_____

_____

_____

_____

_____

_____

Chapter 8
YIELD

In life the YIELD sign can mean many things to different people. Let's focus on the definition of the word. To yield is to give way to pressure or influence. It can also mean to submit to urging or persuasion (Webster's definition). This chapter focuses on not yielding to the things you recognize that are not good for you and responding accordingly. You can also acknowledge that someone else has the right of way to travel by yielding and allowing them to travel first. It is a way of being courteous to other drivers.

On life's journey, we are traveling in the same direction and have the desire to arrive to our destinations safely. A good example is yielding is to let the other driver get ahead by your slowing down. Yielding does not mean you are weak. Yielding could mean you are choosing to take the high road. Yielding can also save you from being delayed. Yielding can mean that you are being cautious and giving other drivers the benefit of doubt.

It's alright to yield in life, just be sure it is going to benefit your trip and not cause you to lose travel time.

YIELD
Write to the Point: Journal Space
(Please use this page to jot down your thoughts after reading this chapter)

Chapter 9
BUMP

Life is full of ups and downs and oftentimes throws us curve balls in the form of death, job loss, divorce, wayward children, evictions, cut-off notices, repossessions, terminal illnesses, incarceration, addictions, loss of a child or parent, …the list goes on and on. BUMPS along the highways of life can be discouraging and cause anyone to want to give up. I am happy to share in this chapter that BUMPS do not mean the end. The scripture reminds us in *Ecclesiastes 3:1 To every thing there is a season, and a time to every purpose under the heaven.*

If not handled properly, bumps can be detrimental to your trip. Slow down, yield if necessary, stop if you must but pay close attention to life's BUMP signs. They could warn you of a speed change. You might just need to slow down to endure the bump and resume the speed you want after the the bump. Don't cause damage to your vehicle because you did not take heed to the sign in life that warned you of the bumps ahead

BUMP
Write to the Point: Journal Space
(Please use this page to jot down your thoughts after reading this chapter)

Chapter 10

NO PARKING – TOW AWAY ZONE

When traveling on highways, there are always designated rest stops for your convenience. The same is true for streets we travel on day in and out. There is signage everywhere advising drivers that "you can't park here". Parking here could cause your vehicle to get towed and this leads to out-of-pocket expenses that were avoidable.

Don't stay on jobs that bring you no satisfaction or where you cannot grow. Don't continue activities that add no love or light to your life. Don't park where you were warned not to. Life could be saying "keep it moving" or "try something new". Don't park anywhere in life where the sign reads NO PARKING – TOW AWAY ZONE. All decisions in life have consequences attached to them; good, bad or indifferent. Be sure you are parking where it is allowed. After all, the meter maids and ticket issuers are watching. You could get towed!

NO PARKING – TOW AWAY ZONE
Write to the Point: Journal Space
(Please use this page to jot down your thoughts after reading this chapter)

_____

_____

_____

_____

_____

_____

_____

_____

_____

_____

_____

_____

_____

Chapter 11
DANGEROUS CURVE AHEAD

You are driving to your next destination and you notice a posted sign that warns "Dangerous Curve Ahead". What should you do when you see this sign? It is in your best interest to prepare to safely approach and drive through the curve. This sign is definitely a warning sign that means there's a sharp curve ahead that requires a slower speed. Pay attention to all warning signs when you are driving.

This warning sign is extremely important because history has proven that when these signs are ignored, it has caused dire consequences up to and including death. Travel well. Travel safe. Some of the seasons we live through in life can be turbulent; however, when approached with caution, drivers can continue on their journey and get to the destinations without incident or accident. Dangerous Curve Ahead, please pay attention and proceed with caution (pun intended).

DANGEROUS CURVE AHEAD
Write to the Point: Journal Space
(Please use this page to jot down your thoughts after reading this chapter)

_____

_____

_____

_____

_____

_____

_____

_____

_____

_____

_____

_____

_____

_____

_____

_____

Chapter 12
KEEP RIGHT

Don't even think about going the opposite way when you see this sign. It is advising you to stay in the direction to the right. Some people get themselves in situations because they refused to comply with the meaning of this sign.

Keep reaching for your goals. Keep asking questions when you are not sure. Keep God first in all you do. Keep praying. Keep fasting. Keep your head up. Keep speaking positive affirmations to yourself and to others. Keep doing what is right even when or if you are tempted to do otherwise. Keep job searching. Keep attending events that bring out the best in you. Keep in touch with your family and friends. Keep living. Keep doing YOU. Keep forgiving yourself and others. Keep letting go and letting God. Keep positive people in your inner circle. Keep being a blessing to others. Keep your focus on people and things that really matter. Keep being grateful.

Next time you see the KEEP RIGHT sign, I pray you will remember this important chapter in *Don't Ignore the Signs!*

KEEP RIGHT
Write to the Point: Journal Space
(Please use this page to jot down your thoughts after reading this chapter)

Chapter 13
DO NOT PASS

Have you ever been driving and out of nowhere, a car passes you in the lane to your left or drives around you abruptly? This is more-than-likely an area on the street where a driver may not have seen the "*Do Not Pass*" sign. When posted, this sign advises drivers to stay put in the current lane.

Do Not Pass means it is probably not safe for you to do so on this stretch of the road. Disobeying this sign could get you a citation or cause you to crash into traffic. Generally, drivers are rushing because they are running late for work or an important meeting. Rushing can cause delays. Rushing can cause drivers to make decisions they would not normally make if they were not trying to beat the clock.

Do Not Pass is posted to warn drivers that it is not safe to pass. Obey the signs. Learn the lessons from past driving mistakes. Some shortcuts are not worthy of the consequences they carry. Set your alarm to leave a little earlier so that rushing and missing *Do Not Pass* signs is not a part of your trip.

DO NOT PASS
Write to the Point: Journal Space
(Please use this page to jot down your thoughts after reading this chapter)

Chapter 14

NO THRU TRAFFIC

This sign is usually posted in a subdivision or business parking lot to warn drivers that it is not to be used as a cut through. In life, this can be liken to the way we allow folks to walk in and out of our lives whenever they so choose. It is imperative to set boundaries in life so that you are not taken for granted. This is also relevant for friendships.

Stop allowing people to only show up in your life when they are in need. If they cannot be a good friend at other times, the friendship probably needs to be re-evaluated. Stop allowing yourself to be taken advantage of. You are in control of who is allowed into your life. Do not continue to complain if you are the one always getting the short end of the stick or left feeling unappreciated in relationships. Make the necessary changes so that you are not always attracting losers. The No Thru Traffic sign is normally posted when complaints have been made by those who live in the area that is being treated like a highway. Pay attention to the signs in your life or you could lose time and energy on unnecessary illegal drivers.

NO THRU TRAFFIC
Write to the Point: Journal Space
(Please use this page to jot down your thoughts after reading this chapter)

_____

_____

_____

_____

_____

_____

_____

_____

_____

_____

_____

_____

_____

_____

Chapter 15
ROAD CLOSED AHEAD

Road Closed Ahead is a warning sign to let drivers know that you should not drive past the sign. Seek an alternate route. Do not keep driving. Do not get distracted and miss this sign. You should treat this sign like a blinking red traffic light that also screams STOP! Continuing to drive after you see the *'Road Closed Ahead'* sign could result in a bad situation for you.

Stop trying to go where you are not invited. Pump the brakes on trying to get people to like you. Some things are just not to be. Do not take it personal. Count it a blessing that God allowed you to see the warning sign. Pull over in a safe area and find out if there is a different route or detour that you can take from where you are.   Do not keep doing things that you know could delay you or hinder your forward progress. The road might be closed for reconstruction or to protect drivers from bad potholes. Whatever the reason, the sign is giving you advance warning that you need to turn around and find a different way to get to your destination.

ROAD CLOSED AHEAD
Write to the Point: Journal Space
(Please use this page to jot down your thoughts after reading this chapter)

_____

_____

_____

_____

_____

_____

_____

_____

_____

_____

_____

_____

_____

_____

Chapter 16
DEAD END

There is a saying "When you know better, you do better" or at least I might add, you should at least try to do better. When driving and you see this sign, you have a number of choices. You can turn around and check the address to make sure you are headed in the right direction or you can obey the sign and know with assurance that this sign is informing you that there is not an exit ahead.

Dead End denotes not going any further. Stay away from dead end jobs, dead end relationships, dead end friendships because they add no value to your life. Stay away from dead end conversations. Do not waste time arguing with people you know just don't get it. Life is meant to be enjoyed. Learn to find ways every day to celebrate life. You do not have time to waste time as you are traveling life's journey.

Don't get caught entertaining foolishness that can also be called Dead End. *Don't Ignore the Signs!* They will save you from losing good energy.

DEAD END
Write to the Point: Journal Space
(Please use this page to jot down your thoughts after reading this chapter)

_____

_____

_____

_____

_____

_____

_____

_____

_____

_____

_____

_____

_____

Chapter 17

EXPECT DELAYS

What a wonderful sign *Expect Delays* can be to those driving to get to a certain destination. When you are forewarned to expect delays, you are being prepared to arrive later than you had planned. Do not allow this warning sign to get you frazzled or nervous. Not all delays are bad ones.

Sometimes delays could be preventing you from potential danger. Breathe. Turn your radio on, listen to some soothing music, and enjoy the ride. In life, you will experience delays even when you have taken the time to plan it all out. Despite planning every detail of your trip (or life), things do not always go as planned. Delays could be God's way of protecting you from something in the future. Here is where your faith needs to take flight.

In life, you will learn that some trips may take longer than planned. It is important to pack your patience so that you are not frustrated with possible delays. Do not let impatience get the best of the good mood that you woke up in. You have to understand that life will not always go as planned. Not everything in life is instant. When setting goals, please understand that things can change along the way. Delays are possible but can be overcome with a positive attitude. Pay attention to the signs as you are driving along life's highways. They are mile markers to assist you in arriving safely with your peace of mind intact.

EXPECT DELAYS
Write to the Point: Journal Space
(Please use this page to jot down your thoughts after reading this chapter)

_____

_____

_____

_____

_____

_____

_____

_____

_____

_____

_____

_____

_____

Chapter 18
DANGEROUS INTERSECTION

This is yet another warning sign that warns you of danger ahead. I pray that after reading to this point, you get the message I am trying to convey and that is to pay careful attention when you are behind the wheel of your life. I believe that God sends signs to prepare us for what is up ahead. When driving and you happen upon this sign, it means just what it says. The intersection you are approaching is a dangerous one. You should proceed with caution and know that your full attention is necessary.

When danger is ahead and we are aware of it, we can prepare better. We can change plans. We can postpone meetings and events had we known trouble was awaiting.

Staying alert and attentive while driving is imperative in life. Don't put yourself in harm's way when you were warned that something out of the ordinary could lie ahead. Life is going to happen with or without our permission. Stay as safe as you can and pay attention to every sign you encounter. On life's highway, you may witness other drivers who are driving without regard for the warning signs, steer clear of them as best you can.

You have so much to live for, so much yet to accomplish. Be prepared to stop, yield and possibly proceed with caution. Your life is speaking…are you listening?

DANGEROUS INTERSECTION
Write to the Point: Journal Space
(Please use this page to jot down your thoughts after reading this chapter)

Chapter 19
DETOUR AHEAD

Detour is defined as a long or roundabout route; usually temporary while construction is taking place. When detour signs are seen, most drivers immediately start looking for the direction in which the detour is as to not miss the appropriate turn to start the detour. Detours take you around the construction or roadwork being completed. Detours can cause delays. Detours can take longer than the normal route you would normally take. Remember that detours don't last always. Once the construction is completed, the streets are open for the normal daily usage.

In our lives, we can admit that our lives have taken detours. Maybe the first marriage did not work out or the first job was just temporary. Whichever the case, faint not, trouble does not last always. Detours also have positive attributes. Detours can teach you patience. Detours teach you that change is inevitable. Detours can nudge you to try something new. Don't be afraid of change. You never know if something will work if you never try it.

Don't get overwhelmed when you experience detours while driving. Stay the course, obey the signs and you will get to a point where you can see your destination just ahead. Yes, your life is still speaking, listen closely.

DETOUR AHEAD
Write to the Point: Journal Space
(Please use this page to jot down your thoughts after reading this chapter)

_____

_____

_____

_____

_____

_____

_____

_____

_____

_____

_____

_____

_____

_____

Chapter 20
LIMITED SIGHT DISTANCE

I must admit, when I chose the signs to use for this book, I was selective in attempting to use what I deemed the most popular signs. One day I passed this particular sign that caught my immediate attention. I slowed down while driving to take notice of everything close to this sign. There were vertical curves right ahead and I decided that day that I would take this route again so that I could take an even closer look on what this sign really meant. I found out through research that this sign warns drivers that you will only be able to see so far ahead of you.

It advises drives that the curves and even hidden driveways may not be visible. Therefore, it is in life, some things in the future, we can't quite see yet. There will be hidden things that you may not quite understand initially but fear not. God specializes in revealing it all to us in his own timing. Be patient as you are driving along. Don't be too busy day or night dreaming that you miss these "not-so-popular" signs. Drive with your faith in tact because there are some things you can only see with your spiritual lenses. Please *Don't Ignore the Signs*!

LIMITED SIGHT DISTANCE
Write to the Point: Journal Space
(Please use this page to jot down your thoughts after reading this chapter)

Chapter 21
REDUCE SPEED AHEAD

The *"reduce speed ahead"* sign indicates that the road you are driving on will shortly have a speed limit change. For example, if you are driving on a road with a limit of 55 mph, a speed zone ahead sign will read "35 zone ahead," which means you must reduce your speed to 35 mph. This sign allows you to anticipate the change and adjust your driving accordingly so you will not be caught going over the limit.

In life, there are times when we are in a hurry and these are the times when we tend to miss what's going on around us. These are the times when we do not take notice of the posted warning signs. You must slow down to allow other drivers to share the road safely. You must slow down to listen to what God is speaking into your life. You must slow down to see the beauty in all things created by God. You must slow down to take it all in. You must slow down to avoid being pulled over by the police. You must slow down to see the warning signs that are ever so present along this journey called life. Pay attention!

REDUCE SPEED AHEAD
Write to the Point: Journal Space
(Please use this page to jot down your thoughts after reading this chapter)

_____

_____

_____

_____

_____

_____

_____

_____

_____

_____

_____

_____

_____

_____

Chapter 22
HILLS AND CURVES

Life is filled with highs, lows, ups, downs, hills and valleys. This warning sign warns drivers that the road will change ahead so that you can prepare properly. Oftentimes, the weather also affects the highway, especially when it rains or snows. If you are speeding, there is no way to judge how sharp curves are or how high hills are. Drivers should slow down and lighten the pressure on brakes until you pass through the curve. Be careful not to brake on hills and curves in your life as it may cause you to skid and this could cause an accident.

When you live through a season of hills and curves, it is a good place to trust God even more. Yes, it is painful and no you do not deserve to have your heart broken over and over again. Nevertheless, isn't comforting to know that trouble doesn't last always? When you are going through a tough time, remember hold onto to your faith and trust the process. Trust the Creator. He knows and sees all. He will carry you through every hill and curve, after all, He is the creator of all things. He made the hills and the curves!

HILLS AND CURVES
Write to the Point: Journal Space
(Please use this page to jot down your thoughts after reading this chapter)

_____

_____

_____

_____

_____

_____

_____

_____

_____

_____

_____

_____

_____

_____

Chapter 23
LIGHTS ON FOR SAFETY

Webster describes safety as the condition of being safe from undergoing or causing hurt, injury, or loss. When the sunsets and daylight becomes nighttime, it is important for drivers to remember to turn the headlights on. You cannot see what lies ahead if you are driving in the dark with no lights. Oncoming traffic cannot see your vehicle and if you are traveling on highway or roadway that is not well lit, you have to practice safety on another level.

The scripture that comes to mind when I decided to include this sign is "I am the light of the world. Whoever follows me will never walk in darkness, but will have the light of life" (John 8:12). The Lord reminds us that He is the light of the world. Why travel in darkness when light proves to be safer? Not to mention, you will probably arrive to your destination safely. Don't be in such a rush that you forget to turn your headlights on. Driving in the dark can be challenging enough. Buckle up and remember safety first!

LIGHTS ON FOR SAFETY
Write to the Point: Journal Space
(Please use this page to jot down your thoughts after reading this chapter)

Chapter 24

DANGER: DO NOT ENTER

A *"Do Not Enter"* sign is usually installed at the beginning of one-way streets, ramps and is posted to prohibit drivers from entering a one-way roadway where traffic is moving in the opposite direction.

A DO NOT ENTER traffic sign is usually installed together with the "WRONG WAY" or "DANGER" signs. What a powerful warning sign that drivers do not need to ignore. Obeying this sign could save your life and the lives of others. Danger lies ahead is the warning this sign gives.

It could be that your life is saying, this is just not for you or please don't waste your time or money. Some describe this as intuition while some may choose to call it a "gut feeling". Normally if something does not feel quite right about something, you should stop, take inventory of all moving parts and make decisions based on your findings. Don't put yourself or those you love in danger's by ignoring the *Danger: Do Not Enter Sign*. Your life is speaking, can't you hear it?

DANGER: DO NOT ENTER
Write to the Point: Journal Space
(Please use this page to jot down your thoughts after reading this chapter)

_____

_____

_____

_____

_____

_____

_____

_____

_____

_____

_____

_____

_____

_____

_____

Chapter 25

CAUTION LANE SHIFT

You are driving along the highway and you start noticing signs that warn you to slow down. You see brake lights ahead of you and you wonder what is going on. You slow down and notice a sign that says *"Caution Lane Shift"* ahead. All of a sudden, the vehicles are starting to shift lanes and you immediately think back to the sign you passed a few miles back.

The sign warned you and other drivers that change was about to take place. Were you prepared? Were you expecting change? Were you paying closer attention? You could spend time planning your life out the way you think it should go. You have prayed, planned and now you are ready to proceed. However, life does not always go as planned. You may end up having to go with plan B. Life can change in the blink of an eye. Don't get left behind because you ignored the sign that your life was about to shift. Be prayerful about where God is taking your life. He will lead and direct you to places unimaginable. Take heed to the signs.

CAUTION LANE SHIFT
Write to the Point: Journal Space
(Please use this page to jot down your thoughts after reading this chapter)

_____

_____

_____

_____

_____

_____

_____

_____

_____

_____

_____

_____

_____

Chapter 26
PHOTO ENFORCED

Watch as well as pray (*Matthew 26:41*) is the scripture that came to mind after seeing this sign several times. These signs are normally located at intersections where the local authorities have installed cameras to monitor that particular stretch of the road. It also reminded me of something I heard growing up "no mater you do, someone's always watching".

As you are driving along, be mindful and attentive to this sign because it also means that some type video recording is also taking place. We live in an age whereby people record everything. Evidence of this can be found on the Internet. I also thought about the saying, "things are not always as they seem".

You can take things in life for face value but be very careful that you are not giving anyone the opportunity to catch you out of character. Someone is watching and waiting to "record" you during your weakest moments. Pay attention to this sign and know when to hold them and when to fold them! Can you hear your life speaking? Listen closely…

PHOTO ENFORCED
Write to the Point: Journal Space
(Please use this page to jot down your thoughts after reading this chapter)

_____

_____

_____

_____

_____

_____

_____

_____

_____

_____

_____

_____

_____

_____

Chapter 27
END SCHOOL ZONE

This sign is seen after you have driven through an area that is considered a school zone. Slower speeds are expected as students and parents are headed to their respective schools. Drivers should be extra careful to obey the school zone speed limits as well as pay attention to any children that may be walking to bus stops. When I decided to use this sign in *Don't Ignore the Signs*, the thought arose that sometimes in life the teachable moments end. You have to take advantage of learning lessons from what life teaches you. Flunk the test and you will have to repeat the test.

Don't give up on furthering your education. It is never too late to start again. It is never too later to pursue a degree. Don't let the END SCHOOL ZONE sign dictate to you when you have to stop pursuing your dreams and goals.

Hard work does pay off. Staying the course has positive benefits. In the words of the elders, "learn all you can and can all you learn". Your life is speaking, tune in.

END SCHOOL ZONE
Write to the Point: Journal Space
(Please use this page to jot down your thoughts after reading this chapter)

Chapter 28

DO NOT BLOCK INTERSECTION

Don't be a hindrance to someone who is trying to move ahead. If you refuse to move on, don't block someone else from leaving. Life is too precious to sit at an intersection because another driver is blocking you from making the turn you need to make. You are not on the roads alone. Don't get in the way of others trying to pursue their dreams. If you cannot encourage and motivate them, you don't need to be in their life. Don't allow others to block your blessings.

Drive with others in mind. Drive with the intent to be as safe as possible. Do not block yourself from moving ahead in life. Traffic is moving along just fine, try not to be a hindrance to other drivers. Be courteous when you are behind the wheel. Don't entertain or respond to any type road rage. Your life is speaking through the signs you see every day. Be vigilant and alert. Keep your eyes and ears open. Your life is speaking! ***Don't Ignore the Signs!***

DO NOT BLOCK INTERSECTION
Write to the Point: Journal Space
(Please use this page to jot down your thoughts after reading this chapter)

Inspirational Scriptures for
DON'T IGNORE THE SIGNS!
Scripture quotations are taken from the King James and
NIV versions of the Bible

I praise you because I am fearfully and wonderfully made
(Psalm 139:14)

*There is a way that appears to be right, but in the end it leads
to death.*
(Proverbs 14:12)

*And he shall be like a tree planted by the rivers of water,
that bringeth forth his fruit in his season; his leaf also shall
not wither; and whatsoever he doeth shall prosper.*
Psalm 1:3 (KJV)

A friend loves at all times.
(Proverbs 17:17)

*But seek first his kingdom and his righteousness, and all these
things will be given to you as well.*
(Matthew 6:33)

*The LORD himself goes before you and will be with you; he
will never leave you nor forsake you. Do not be afraid; do not
be discouraged.*
(Deuteronomy 31:8)

*And we know that all things work together for good to them that
love God, to them who are the called according to his purpose.*
(Romans 8:28)

DON'T IGNORE THE SIGNS!
Scripture quotations are taken from the King James and
NIV versions of the Bible

Trust in the Lord with all thine heart; and lean not to thine own understanding. In all thy ways acknowledge Him and He shall direct thy paths.
(Proverbs 3:5-6)

Wait on the Lord and be of good courage and the Lord will strengthen thine heart, wait, I say, on the Lord.
(Psalm 27:14)

Let us not become weary in doing good, for at the proper time we will reap a harvest if we do not give up.
(Galatians 6:9)

The Lord is not slack concerning his promise, as some men count slackness; but is longsuffering to us-ward, not willing that any should perish, but that all should come to repentance
(2 Peter 3:9)

I will lift my eyes to the hills from where my help comes.
(Psalm 121:1)

Being confident of this very thing, that he which hath begun a good work in you will perform it until the day of Jesus Christ.
(Phillippians 1:6)

Weeping may endure for a night but JOY comes in the morning.
(Psalm 30:5)

Acknowledgements

I am forever grateful that I am the chosen vessel to pen my second book, *Don't Ignore the Signs!* I do not take my life or gifts for granted. I will always remember that every good and perfect gift comes from the Most High. (*James 1:17*)

I remain sincerely appreciative of those who continue to support my dream of being an author. My prayer is that I will always make you proud to know and love me.

My Family: From near and far, I am extremely blessed with family members who have consistently encouraged and uplifted me. I am grateful for each of you.

My Children: **Courtney and LaMonte',** my love for you is truly endless. Witnessing your adulthood is a wonderful blessing as your MOM. I will always support your dreams and goals. Remember to always keep God first and pray about EVERYTHING. Mommy will always be in your corner.

My Dad (Charles Moore) and stepmom (Anita). *Happy 50th Wedding anniversary*! May God grant you more years of togetherness, happiness and prosperity.

To my siblings**, Darryl, Michelle, Alysia, William and Jared,** I thank God for our bond. To our brother **William**, your time is coming baby and we will be here to embrace and love on you like never before. In the words of our Dad, "All Good Stuff". We are indeed Charlie's Angels.

To my God Mom **Clotele Berrian**. Your strength and love continues to amaze me. I am blessed beyond measure to have you in my life and I love you endlessly.

To **Carlito Miaz:** Thank you for always listening to me read chapters of my book projects and offering honest critique. Thank you for your patience, love, support and encouragement from day one. In the voice of the late maestro Teddy Pendergrass, *"It feels good loving somebody when somebody loves you back"*.

To my god brother, **Devione Linder**, I am so peacock proud of the man you are becoming. Worthy is watching from Heaven. I am willing to bet that she is just as proud of you. I will always be 'Auntie Shunda' to you and I will always love you. **Bernotta Linder**, please continue to take good care of my Mom's big baby.

My **(Forever) Friends:** Thank you for being true P*roverbs 17:17* friends in my life. I am so grateful for your love and endless support: Michelle Hill, Angela Young-Davis, Vivian Webb, Katrinda McQueen, Sonya Marable, Tonya Pitts, Phyllis White, Todra Washington, Geraldine Brown, Millicent Crawford, Shirley Straughter, Jennifer Copeland, Hannah Jackson, Debra Washington Bradley, Alma H. McCoy, Robert B. Mitchell, Kennedy Cooper and Jonathan Bellamy. I will forever cherish our friendships.

I am appreciative for new friendships that continue to evolve in my life. Some of you I met during the course of my completing *"Do Something New!"* while others I met since that time. I just want to remind you that you are special in my life. **Forever thanks** to Christy Wrape', Michael Woodard, Pastor Vernell Henry, Evangelist Tracy Robinson, Evangelist Crystal Butler, Angela Myers-Cooper, JL King, Katrice Barnes, Kilby Lamar, Timothy Keys, Christopher Washington, Sonya Davis, Dawn Hernandez, Laura

McCombs, Mary Beth Cleveland, Andora Robinson, Machille Johnson Harvest, Cecile Mitchell, Diane Hart, Deborah Morrison, Virginia Johnson, Egele and Egile Morrison, Rylan Downing, Shonta Clark-Bass, Paula Jones, John and Tammy Tooley, Asia Knowles, Laura Foster, Annette Newman, Darlene Davis, Anthony Rollerson, Kimberly Boykin, Lisa R. Straughter, Andrea Moore Rucker, Mia Moore and Loretta Dixon Jones.

My Classmates: To each of you who continue to give from the heart to be a blessing to others. I am extremely proud to be forever connected to an awesome group of friends. To one of the **best** graduating classes of *Valdosta High School (Class of 1983),* I pause to extend sincere gratitude and to tell you that I love each of you forever. Let's stay together.

To the Southside and Friends Reunion Committee. Thanks for running with the vision and for keeping childhood friends together. **Special thanks** to Bernie and Barbara Gaines, Darryl and Michelle Brown, Julie Harris, Evelyn Wright, Tonia J. Singleton, Malisa Williams-Harris, Obeatrice Simmons, Tonia J. Singleton, Jennifer Tooley and Darrell Battle.

In this lifetime, we meet incredible people on this journey who remind us that God's love is truly infinite. For all the respect and honor you extend to and for me, I am humbly grateful. I love you all and I am proud of you for working hard to take care of yourselves and to make it do what it do! **Heartfelt thanks** to: Scottie McPherson, Perisha Smith, Ju'won L. Jackson, Monica Mcbroom, Satira Njie, Tiara Donald, Jacelyn (Joc Jose), Isaiah S. Freeman, Derrick Bryant, Novoa Champion, Paul Hopson and Vanessa Hundley.

To my **Pastor & First Lady, Elders Darryl and Juakena Winston,** you will always be dear to me. Thanks for seeing and believing in my potential and for always encouraging me to be the BEST. To the members of **Greater Works Assembly,** thank you for your endless love and support. Continue to rest in peace *Elder Gwendolyn G. Godfrey. (12/19/14), Deacon Norris E. Williams* (9/11/16), and *Evangelist Lugene Godfrey Childs (07/02/18)*, your love and legacies will always be remembered and respected by the Greater Works family.

A special thank you to several women and men of God of the cloth who continue to influence my life in a major way. Love and appreciation to **Elder Otis M. Rawls, Pastor Cynthia Robinson, Pastor Alfred A. Miller, Apostle Julia G. Berry, Evangelist Rosa L. Thomas-Webb** and **Rev. Dr. Bennie E. Calloway III** and the late **Bishop Larry E. Boston.** I pray God's choice blessings for you and everyone connected to your lives.

I thank **everyone** who played a role, no matter how small or large in supporting my dreams. This second book is truly God inspired and ordained and I'm expecting very favorable feedback as readers embrace it.

A few weeks before the completion of this book, I was involved in what could have been a fatal car accident. I know that God spared my life and I am forever grateful for the assigned angels of protection. ***Don't Ignore the Signs*** gained a new level of dedication after seeing my life flash before my eyes. I praise God for His keeping power. The best is yet to come!

DON'T IGNORE THE SIGNS!

Questions to consider by chapter

No U Turn (Page 9)
- What did this chapter bring to mind?
- Have you ever needed to make a U-turn in your life?
- How did you move forward from the U-turn?

STOP (Page 12)
- What did this chapter bring to mind?
- Is there anything you need to STOP currently?
- Will you make the necessary changes to STOP?

Do Not Enter (Page 16)
- What did this chapter bring to mind?
- Have there been times when you ignored the signs that read "Do Not Enter"?
- Will you pay more attention to this sign after having read Chapter 3?

Slow (Page 18)
- What did this chapter bring to mind?
- Are you a patient person or is your attention span very short?
- Do you like rushing or do you like to take your time and get things right the first time?

Wrong Way (Page 20)
- What did this chapter bring to mind?
- Have you ever traveled or driven the wrong way?
- How did you get back on track after going the wrong way?

DON'T IGNORE THE SIGNS!

Questions to consider by chapter

Stay in Lane (Page 23)

- What did this chapter bring to mind?
- Is it frustrating to you when others get outside of what they are called and gifted to do? Explain.
- How do you plan on staying in your lane?

Proceed with Caution (Page 26)

- What did this chapter bring to mind?
- Have you ever ignored the "Proceed with Caution" sign? What were the results?
- Are you willing to take your time to arrive safer now that you've read this chapter?

Yield (Page 28)

- What did this chapter bring to mind?
- Are there times in your life when you need to yield?
- What areas in your life are affected when you decide to yield?

Bump (Page 30)

- What did this chapter bring to mind?
- Have you ever experienced life's bumps?
- How did you handle the "bumps"?

No Parking – Tow Away Zone (Page 32)

- What did this chapter bring to mind?
- Have you ever ignored a No Parking sign?
- What were the results of not obeying this sign?

DON'T IGNORE THE SIGNS!

Questions to consider by chapter

Dangerous Curve Ahead (Page 34)

- What did this chapter bring to mind?
- Have you ever felt like you were warned of trouble ahead?
- How do you handle life's dangerous curves?

Keep Right (Page 36)

- What did this chapter bring to mind?
- Have you ever had to encourage yourself to keep going? To stay the course?
- Can you now help someone else who may need to keep the faith and keep it moving?

Do Not Pass (Page 38)

- What did this chapter bring to mind?
- Have you ever felt that you needed to stay put for now? Explain.
- Have you learned anything from this chapter?

No Thru Traffic (Page 40)

- What did this chapter bring to mind?
- Have you ever felt your kindness was taken for granted?
- Are you now able and willing to be honest about your feelings to others?

Road Closed Ahead (Page 42)

- What did this chapter bring to mind?
- Do you obey signs that warn of road closures?
- Are you willing to take detours when roads are closed due to construction?

DON'T IGNORE THE SIGNS!

Questions to consider by chapter

Dead End (Page 44)

- What did this chapter bring to mind?
- Have you encountered dead end relationships?
- How did you handle these type relationships?

Expect Delays (Page 46)

- What did this chapter bring to mind?
- Do you consider delays aggravating?
- Do you adjust and adapt easily to whatever is going on? Why or why not?

Dangerous Intersection (Page 49)

- What did this chapter bring to mind?
- Have you ever ignored this type sign?
- How did you handle a warning of danger ahead?

Detour Ahead (Page 52)

- What did this chapter bring to mind?
- Do you get upset when a detour is necessary?
- What did you gain from reading this chapter?

Limited Sight Distance (Page 55)

- What did this chapter bring to mind?
- Do you walk by faith or by what you see?
- What is your definition of "vision"?

Reduce Speed Ahead (Page 57)

- What did this chapter bring to mind?
- Do you obey the "slow down" posted signs?
- What have you learned from slowing down in a fast-paced world?

DON'T IGNORE THE SIGNS!

Questions to consider by chapter

Hills and Curves (Page 59)

- What did this chapter bring to mind?
- How do you respond to life's hills and curves?
- Can you help others who are dealing with life's hills and curves? How would you help them?

Lights on for Safety (Page 61)

- What did this chapter bring to mind?
- Do you ever forget to turn your headlights on?
- What would you say is safe about having your lights on?

Danger: Do Not Enter (Page 63)

- What did this chapter bring to mind?
- What encounters have you experienced with danger while driving?
- Have you stayed away from dangerous situations before being warned?

Caution Lane Shift (Page 65)
- What did this chapter bring to mind?
- Do you recognize when things are shifting in your life?
- How do you handle change in your life?

Photo Enforced (Page 67)

- What did this chapter bring to mind?
- Are you encouraged to be aware of your surroundings after reading this chapter?
- What encouragement can you offer as it relates to knowing that people are watching?

DON'T IGNORE THE SIGNS!

Questions to consider by chapter

End School Zone (Page 69)

- What did this chapter bring to mind?
- Are you still learning on this life journey?
- Are you willing to teach what you have learned?

Do Not Block Intersection (Page 71)

- What did this chapter bring to mind?
- Are you a blessing blocker? Do you help others reach their goals?
- How do you encourage others not to block intersections in life?

And Finally...

I choose to end **Don't Ignore the Signs** with these precious girls. They are special gifts in my life that I love and adore. I am convinced that God healed by broken heart over losing my MOM when these precious babies' were born.

Dimeon Shayyla Latrice Lester (4 years old) and
Kristian Reign Latrice Ponder, (2 years old),
my little angels on earth.
(This book is dedicated to them)
Always remember that you can be anything you
want to be in life. Aim for the stars!

"Grammy's babies"
Dimeon Shayyla Latrice & Kristian Reign Latrice

Made in the USA
Middletown, DE
21 September 2022

10372108R10049